Executive Summary

OPERATION RESTORE HOPE, the United States-led operation in Somalia, began on the 9th of December 1992. The United States-led mission was designated United Nations Task Force Somalia (UNITAF). UNITAF was given the full political support of the United Nations, but the operation would be planned and executed by the United States. This comparative analysis will examine the role of OAS operations in support of UNITAF and UNOSOM II. OAS engagements in Somalia were limited, but the presence of OAS aircraft greatly impacted ground operations. Additionally, I will examine the use of the JFACC during UNITAF operations and the command and control system used by UNOSOM II. In August of 1992, the United States provided logistic support and established a Joint Task Force (JTF), designated OPERATION PROVIDE RELIEF, in conjunction with the formation of UNOSOM. UNOSOM and OPERATION PROVIDE RELIEF would yield to UNITAF/OPERATION RESTORE HOPE in December of 1992. UNITAF, in May of 1993, would turn the mission back to the United Nations under UNOSOM II. The transfer of the mission from a United States-led and equipped force to a United Nations led and equipped force would cause a myriad of challenges.

OPERATION RESTORE HOPE, the United States-led operation in Somalia, began on the 9th of December 1992. Thus began one of the most controversial and precedent setting operations in United States foreign policy and military history. The United States-led mission was designated United Task Force Somalia (UNITAF). UNITAF was given the full political support of the United Nations, but the operation would be planned and executed by the United States. The United Nations had previously attempted to restore peace and end the starvation that plagued the east African nation. The United Nations mission in Somalia (UNOSOM), which had begun in the fall of 1992, had fallen critically short of providing either the necessary entry force or adequate humanitarian sustainment to complete the assigned mission under United Nations resolutions. The United States had provided logistic support and established a Joint Task Force (JTF), designated OPERATION PROVIDE RELIEF, in conjunction with the formation of UNOSOM. A critical weakness within UNOSOM and OPERATION PROVIDE RELIEF was their ability to project significant air power. UNOSOM and OPERATION PROVIDE RELIEF would yield to UNITAF/OPERATION RESTORE HOPE in December of 1992.

UNITAF forces would operate under chapter VII of the United Nations Charter to create a secure environment for the delivery of humanitarian aid using all necessary military means. UNITAF leadership would place great emphasis on the use of offensive air support (OAS) for independent and in support of ground operations. UNITAF, in May of 1993, would turn the mission back to the United Nations under UNOSOM II.

The transfer of the mission from a United States-led and equipped force to a United Nations led and equipped force would cause a myriad of challenges. The lack of air forces and an expanding mission for UNOSOM II would lead to several decisive engagements with the Somali militias. This comparative analysis will examine the role of OAS operations in support of UNITAF and UNOSOM II. OAS engagements in Somalia were limited, but the presence of OAS aircraft greatly impacted ground operations. This analysis will look at OAS assets available, command and control, doctrine and command relationships within UNITAF and UNOSOM II. Additionally, the role of the UNITAF Joint Force Air Component Commander (JFACC) will be analyzed along with the Joint/Combined air-planning cell, which replaced the JFACC during UNOSOM II

<u>Historical Setting</u>

From a United States perspective, the theater was under the purview of the United States Central Command (CENTCOM), commanded by General Joseph P. Hoar. Somalia is located on the horn of Africa and was once considered to hold key geostrategic relevance (see figure1).

The nation had been in the midst of a civil war. The civil war had led to the departure of then President Major General Said Barre. His departure was accelerated amid defeat from rival clan leaders. Somalia had been both a United States and Soviet ally over the 20 years preceding the civil war. The Soviet influence ended in the late 1970s. The Somali/ Soviet relationship was a symbiotic relationship of weapons for geostrategic reach. The spread of Soviet influence and Islamic extremist had led then president Jimmy Carter to establish CENTCOM. CENTCOM, located in Tampa,

Florida, provided a United States presence and formed strategic alliances throughout

Africa and the Persian Gulf. The 1980's saw increased United States military and

economic aid to Africa, which created infrastructure in the long-term hopes of political

and economic reform.

The civil war of 1979 had allowed for the formation of several factional groups within

Somalia.[1] General Mohamed Farah Aideed led one of the most active and militant

parties. Aideeds party, which had been instrumental in the defeat of Barre, was the

political arm of the Somali National Alliance (SNA), the United Somali Congress (USC).

Aideed would become the primary political voice of Mogadishu, the capital. His primary

rival in Mogadishu would be Somali businessman Ali Mahdi Mohamed. Two major

factions also controlled Southern Somalia. Colonel Omar Jess was a member of the

Somali Patriotic Movement (SPM) and was fighting the son-in-law of Said Barre, General Said Hersi Morgan. Colonel Jess was aligned with Aideed in Mogadishu.

The United States-led intervention in Somalia, which began in August of 1992, was a result of the continued fighting combined with draught and famine. The end state for the factions was control of the two major cities in Somalia, Mogadishu and Kismayo. The United States-led intervention was a follow-on force. The initial humanitarian mission, United Nations Somalia (UNOSOM), had begun under United Nations Security Council Resolution 751 on April 24th 1992.[2] Prior to the establishment of UNOSOM, the United Nation had passed resolution 733, which created an arms embargo, "saying it was gravely alarmed at the rapid deterioration of the situation in Somalia and the heavy loss of human life and widespread material damage."[3] This embargo was a source of friction for both Ali Mahdi and Aideed. The Secretary-General of the United Nations, Boutros Boutros-Ghali invited both parties to New York and talks began on the 12th of February 1992. The two sides agreed to a general cease-fire, but Ali Mahdi was unsuccessful at getting the United Nations to commit a peacekeeping force. Ali Mahdi was untrusting of Aideed and wary of Aideed's increasing power. This led to Security Council resolution 746, which supported United Nations humanitarian work to continue along with a "technical team".

Offensive Air support

At this point an explanation of the OAS mission in Somalia is necessary. The use of the term OAS may be deceiving in the context of UNITAF and UNOSOM II

---

[1] To better understand the history of the conflict in Somalia and the United States political role in both UNITAF and UNOSOM II see *Somalia and Operation Restore Hope* by John Hirsh and Robert Oakley.
[2] For a complete listing of all United Nations resolutions and their specific mandates see The United Nations in Somalia 1992-1996 produced by the United Nations Department of Public Information.

operations. OAS was used primarily as a deterrent or a show-of-force. The OAS employment was initially designed for traditional combat missions. The JFACC would tailor the use of OAS to include presence missions. It became apparent to UNITAF planners that OAS assets were a credible deterrent to the Somalis.

The initial phases of UNITAF were dominated by naval aviation conducting OAS missions. Other Joint and United Nations air forces would provide limited amounts of OAS assets. The United States Army would provide a significant amount of attack helicopter assets during both UNITAF and UNOSOM II operations. The 10th Mountain division would operate their attack battalion as an independent maneuver element for the majority of UNITAF operations. The United States Army's 160th Special Operations Aviation regiment (SOAR) would operate during the later stages of UNOSOM II in support of Rangers and Delta Force. OAS is "those air operations conducted against enemy installations, facilities, and personnel to directly assist the attainment of MAGTF objectives by the destruction of enemy resources or the isolation of his military force."[4] OAS is one of the six primary functions of Marine aviation. Marine aviation is specifically trained and equipped to operate in support of the MAGTF. Marine aviation further subsets OAS into deep (DAS) and close (CAS) air support. Both DAS and CAS are accepted terms and procedures within Joint doctrine.

CAS is defined as air action by fixed- and rotary-wing aircraft against hostile targets, which are in, close proximity to friendly forces and which require detailed integration of each air mission with the fire and movement of those forces.[5] Finally, DAS is air action against enemy targets at such distance from friendly forces that detailed

---

[3] United Nations, *The Blue Helmets* (New York: United Nations, 1998), 288.
[4] MCRP 5-12C, Marine Corps Supplement to the DOD Dictionary of Military and Associated Terms

integration of each mission with fire and movement of friendly forces is not required.

Deep air support missions are flown on either side of the fire support coordination line;

the lack of a requirement for close coordination with the fire and movement of friendly

forces is the qualifying factor. DAS missions include strike coordination, air interdiction,

and armed reconnaissance.[6] The initial capabilities of the air forces[7] of UNITAF would

dominate the ground scheme of maneuver. The lack of assets and integration of OAS

assets with UNOSOM II forces would be become a significant limitation.

Operation Provide Relief

CENTCOM had begun support for Somalia in earnest with the deployment of the

Humanitarian Assistance Survey Team (HAST). This team had evolved through

planning at CENTCOM with the Agency for International Development (AID) and the

Office for Foreign Disaster Assistance of the Department of State.[8] CENTCOM had

designated I Marine Expeditionary Force (I MEF) as the JTF for contingency operations.

The HAST was established on August 16, 1992. Brigadier General Frank Libutti,

USMC, who was serving at CENTCOM, would lead the JTF.[9] The mission was critical

to the development of air operations into Somalia. The use of aviation assets would

establish the groundwork for the UNITAF intervention.

OPERATION PROVIDE RELIEF would organize using non-traditional

componency relationships. The mission was completely based on heavy airlift; there was

---

[5] Joint Publication 1-02, DOD Dictionary of Military and Associated Terms
[6] Organization of Marine Corps Forces, MCRP 5-12D, 1998, chapter 3
[7] For a complete explanation of the six functions of Marine Corps aviation see MAWTS-1 website, under www.usmc.mil look under units and mission.
[8] For more information concerning OPERATION PROVIDE RELIEF see the book *Rogue Ambassador* written by Ambassador Smith Hempstone, the former United States Ambassador to Kenya.
[9] Frank Libutti, Commanding General of Fleet Marine Forces Pacific, interviewed by author, 8 December 2000. Libutti served as the Joint Task Force commander, OPERATION PROVIDE RELIEF. General

little consideration for the use of OAS assets. The planning for air assets was through a centralized airlift coordination committee.[10] CENTCOM insisted the mission be measurable and attainable. Though primarily a logistic airlift operating from Mombassa, Kenya, Libutti demanded protection of the humanitarian relief aircraft and aircrews once the flights arrived outlying Somali airfields. This was accomplished through the use of United States Army Special Forces. Special Forces were embarked, as a security force, into a second or third aircraft and orbit above the airfield. If the Non-Governmental Organization (NGO) or aircrew were threatened while delivering the relief supplies the security force could be landed. The mission laid the basic requirements for UNITAF and highlighted the need for a strong political campaign with the Somalis. It also highlighted the requirement to provide overwhelming force verse sufficient force. The lessons learned by UNOSOM and OPERATION PROVIDE RELIEF would highlight the need for the extensive use of tactical aviation to provide OAS. The challenges that Libutti faced were extensive. Force protection was necessary for each mission and the lack of security is what kept relief supplies from arriving at the international airport in Mogadishu.

The PROVIDE RELIEF mission was designed to deliver relief supplies, working through NGOs, into southern Somalia and northern Kenya.[11] The mission would be closely coordinated with NGOs. The NGOs and the JTF were concentrating their effort on southern Somali villages. It was evident to the JTF that Mogadishu and the southern

---

Joseph Hoar, USMC, CINCCENT assigned him as the JTF Commander. Libutti served on the CENTCOM staff in the J-5 and arrived in Mombassa, Kenya as the JTF Commander on 12 August 1992.
[10] Libutti interview
[11] The Kenyan government allowed United States C-130 and C-141 aircraft to operate from Mombassa provided they delivered relief supplies to famine stricken portions of northern Kenya prior to operations in Somalia. Only USAF (active duty, reserve and National Guard) C-130s flew into Somalia due to the lengths and condition of the runways.

port city of Kismayo were the centers of gravity. Who ever were expected to control Somalia needed to control these two cities. They were the two legitimate sources of strength in the nation; the two cities were strategic centers of gravity and did not change throughout the conflict. With such an importance being placed on the cities combined with a lack of dedicated OAS assets and limited numbers of security forces available, the risk was deemed unacceptable to fly relief supplies into these cities. The JTF worked closely with the NGOs and the Somali clan leaders to reduce tensions. Libutti met with both Ali Mahdi and Aideed to explain the JTFs mission. The JTFs mission of providing relief supplies would soon be outpaced by the political concerns of both the United Nations and its members. The United Nations mission (UNOSOM) was struggling to put its arms around the scope and complexity of the mission.

OPERATION PROVIDE RELIEF set the operational stage for military intervention in Somalia. Though the mission success had little impact on the United States decision to expand its role [12], it did highlight the need for a role of OAS for an expanded mission. The decision to expand the mission would demand that forces address the centers of gravity. The increased United Nations and United States presence would, by December of 1992, demand additional combat forces. A key to these forces would be mobility and firepower. The operation and the JTF would complete their mission in November of 1992. The continuing mission in Mogadishu had been established under UNOSOM and coordination between the OPERATION PROVIDE RELIEF JTF and UNOSOM was continuous, but the priority would shift back to the UNOSOM mission and the deterioration of the mission in Mogadishu.

United Nations Commitment Expands

It was the deterioration of Mogadishu which led to the Secretary-General's initial decision to allow for the "establishment of the United Nations Operations in Somalia (UNOSOM), comprising of 50 military observers to monitor the cease-fire, and a 500-strong infantry unit to provide sufficiently strong military escort to deter attack and to fire effectively in self-defense if deterrence should not be effective."[13]   This action would be authorized under Security Council resolution 751 on 24 April 1992. Pakistani General Shaheen would be the chief military observer and would lead the UNOSOM military mission. He would quickly realize that he was unable to cope with the escalating violence and increasing demands on his limited force. Through a series of Security Council Resolutions, including 755, "the number of troops authorized rose to 4200 by September of 1992. UNOSOM troops would come under increasing fire from General Aideed through November, including 8 killed."[14]

The United Nations was soon at a crossroads and the tactical situation was spiraling out of control. The United Nations had no organic rotary or fixed wing attack aircraft easily available to support ground operations. The lack of OAS would put UNOSOM troops at a distinct disadvantage. Their daily patrols would be competing with Somali desires to control the city. UNOSOM troops were being portrayed by Aideed and Ali Mahdi as imperialistic and met with increasing resistance. Somalia had no legitimate government and no police force. The Security Council concluded, "it was time to move into Chapter VII of the Charter and asked him (the Secretary-General) for specific

---

[12] Libutti interview. LtGen Libutti reported his experiences to the Chairman of the Joint Chiefs of Staff (CJCS) General Colin Powell and the J3 in November of 1992. The plans for OPERATION RESTORE HOPE had already begun.

[13] United Nations, 290.

recommendations".[15]   The apparent solution came in the form of a proposal by the former United States Secretary of State Lawrence Eagleberger. The United States had offered to act as an authorized member state of the United Nations to protect humanitarian relief efforts in Somalia.

This was a major shift in the operations in Somalia. The United States had proposed to take the lead in providing the secure environment in which humanitarian aid could be administered. The United States would embark on this campaign with the will of the American people and a well trained and led American military. The decision for the United States to become involved came after major news sources reported the wide spread starvation and famine to the world. The pictures of starvation were not new to the American public. However, these photographs and videos combined with 'bandits' roaming the streets and the slaughter of women and children brought widespread public outcry. This led to the decision by then President George H.W. Bush, in August 1992, to increase airlifts of humanitarian aid into Somalia.

The United States campaign in Somalia would be planned at the highest levels. The Bush administration appeared concerned with both public and international opinion. "It was apparent at this point that the Joint Chiefs Chairman Colin Powell took the lead in the Defense department's decision to propose a large-scale United States military intervention, going considerably further than the JCS staff had originally been prepared to go."[16]   The lead for the plans quickly fell onto CENTCOM. The political impact of intervention in Somalia was, as previously mentioned, twofold. The Bush administration

---

[14] United Nations, 721.
[15] United Nations, 293.
[16] John Hirsh and Robert Oakley, *Somalia and Operation Restore Hope* (Washington, D.C.: United States Institute for Peace, 1995), 42.

would be perceived as acting decisively and forcefully. The administration would allow the military enough flexibility to provide the right force mix and commit them quickly which, "might help offset the widespread criticism that the United States was dilatory in responding to aggression in Bosnia."[17]

The United Nations had more than 16 countries participating in UNOSOM. These nations were mandated to provide troops and equipment per United Nations charter. Yet, these forces had little offensive capability[18]. They lacked integrated fire support and had no operational mobility and limited tactical mobility. To the participating nations, there were no vital interests at stake. This lack of support was not atypical for previous United Nations missions. Never had participating countries provided air mobility in support of operations nor had they provided OAS assets. The shift into Chapter VII was a large leap from traditional United Nations roles; the mission under UNOSOM was designed and manned as most other United Nation missions were organized worldwide.

The uniqueness of the Somali situation was highlighted by the lack of an established and functioning government. This lack of political infrastructure increased the need for forces along with associated command and control. The Somali nation had no formal trading links with the international community. The country was completely dependent on international aid. The people of Somalia were generally unaware of any Somali national vital interests. The majority of Somalis are nomadic herders or farmers and the draught and famine, which had extended into 1992, had killed nearly 2 million of them.

---

[17] Hirsh and Oakley, 42.

The warring factions were the only organizations who stood to lose with foreign intervention. Up to this point, the factions had been successful at intercepting and re-selling aid. The factions had been able to import arms and currency, and profit from a growing black market. The factions could hardly recognize vital national interests; they were concerned with self-preservation and the possibility of increased power.

Somalia's Continuing Decline thru 1992

Somalia had been subjected to a power vacuum since the final defeat and departure of Said Barre. The Somalis had enjoyed a relatively robust military, but the extended famine combined with internal and external strife had taken its toll. Their two-year war with Ethiopia, which ended in 1978, was costly and led to the downfall of Said Barre. Though by 1992 there was no formal military, but there was a cadre of trained and seasoned military officers. These soldiers would begin to form the backbone of Aideed's guerilla army[19]. The primary goal of Aideed was to seize power with the help of the United Nations. If he could convince the United States and the United Nations that he was responsible and responsive to input, he could emerge as the next leader of Somalia. His goal throughout the mission of UNOSOM was to discourage the United Nations force, but he would change tactics once UNITAF was formed and again revert once UNOSOM II assumed the mission.

Aideed knew that Mogadishu was the center of gravity of Somalia. If he could control the city, than he could control the nation. With that in mind, Aideed was able to continue to stockpile weapons and organize his militia. The majority of the militia was either from the same clan, hired guns or members of the SNA. Aideed's forces were well

---

[18] Joshua Siani, *United Nations Peacekeeping: Lessons Learned* (Washington, D.C.: Library of Congress, 1994), 285-87.

trained in guerilla tactics and understood the basics of the urban fight. The force did not need to be well trained to succeed. These forces grew more confident after observing and attacking UNOSOM forces. This would change almost immediately upon the arrival of UNITAF.

The intent of the United States special envoy, Robert Oakley, was to explain to Aideed and Ali Mahdi what would be expected of them. Oakley also brought with him the OPERATION PROVIDE RELIEF JTF Commander, Brigadier General Frank Libutti, to the talks.[20] Oakley articulated the need for Somali forces to avoid confrontation with United States forces. This message was successful as seen from the unopposed landing of Marines and SEALs on December 9th 1992. This use of military and political instruments of power was very successful. Oakley understood the need and requirement for the use of OAS platforms. He went so far as to have F-14A *Tomcat* fighter aircraft from the USS Ranger and   AH-1W *SuperCobra* attack helicopters form the USS Tripoli conduct flyovers and show of force maneuvers. These flights were conducted during the meetings with Aideed and Ali Mahdi.[21] Oakley had quickly realized that the Somalis were fearful of attack aircraft. The use of fixed and rotary wing attack aircraft as psychological weapons would continue throughout OPERATION RESTORE HOPE. The militia under Aideed would continue to gather popular support throughout UNITAFs deployment but would limit their challenges to United States and United Nations military forces.

United Task Force Somalia, December 1992

---

[19] Sinai, 283.
[20] Libutti interview.
[21] Libutti interview.

The UNITAF forces would be consolidated under Lieutenant General Robert B. Johnston, the Commanding General of I MEF and his chain of command was directly to CENTCOM. The Special Envoy, Oakley reported directly back to the State Department. The pairing of these two would be fortuitous for UNITAF. The establishment of open dialogues between the United Nations, existing NGOs, the media, participating nations and the Somalis was impressive. Oakley would be a key player in guiding the United Nations Special Envoy Kittani. Kittani had been previously designated the United Nations special envoy to Somalia, but lacked the real power that only Oakey enjoyed. Kittani was the person empowered to make decisions for the United Nations with the Somalis, but Oakley was clearly the person with the experience and support of United States forces. This would become a source of friction for the UNITAF mission. It would not take long for the Somalis to realize that Oakley not Kittani was the powerbroker.

Local attitudes towards the United States and the United Nations had begun to diverge, sometimes rather awkwardly. Not only did the United States military presence overshadow the United Nations' by early 1993, but also the perception of the United States as the remaining international superpower affected the response of Somali leaders. It was perhaps inevitable that Aideed and Ali Mahdi, jockeying for future political position, looked to Oakley as the principal interlocutor on the broader issues facing Somalia.[22]

The strategic mission of UNITAF would be a built around a four-phased operation. "The United States Central Command, which was in charge of the combined operation, was following a four-phased programme to realize the objectives of securing major airports and seaports, key installations and food distribution points, and providing open and free passage of relief supplies, with security for convoys and relief organizations and those supplying humanitarian relief."[23] The United States was determined to end the famine and starvation in Somalia by protecting the humanitarian workers. The mission marked a change in the strategic mindset of the United States in their support of United Nations missions.

In the recent past, the United States had been reluctant to support the United Nations with American troops. However, the mission in Somalia could be tailored to fit into the newly developed Powell Doctrine. The recent success of the United States military in the 1991 Persian Gulf War was a good example of the use of overwhelming force. The logical follow-on was the application of this overwhelming force and its associated technology to support the mission in Somalia. This mission was viewed by the NSC as a " do-able" mission. According to the NSC, the mission could be accomplished and would have a definable beginning and end. The mission would also have defined rules of engagement (ROE)[24] that would support the soldier's ability to accomplish the mission. The United States clearly planned to return the mission back to the United Nations once order had been restored, but this was not fully accepted by the United Nations. In a letter from the Secretary-General Boutros Boutros-Ghali, he urged President Bush to expand the mission to disarming Somalis; "It would be a tragedy if the premature departure of the United Task Force were to plunge Somalia back into anarchy

---

[22] Hirsh and Oakley, 50.

[23] United Nations, 295.

[24] The Rules of Engagement (ROE) for United States military forces in support of Operation Restore Hope/UNITAF were designed to be adaptable to the changing tactical situation. The ROE supported the UNITAF mission and ROE failures were limited to two documented cases. The ROE for UNISOM II represented the expanded mandate of UNOSOM II into Chapter VII and peace enforcement. The ROE included all crew served weapons and allowed for the active disarmament of Somalis. This expanded mandate would have grave implications for Task Force Ranger in October of 1993. For more information see Hirsh and Oakley.

and starvation"[25]. The NSC rejected the proposal by the Secretary-General. This plea would plant the seed for a requirement of a United States manned and led quick reaction force (QRF) during UNOSOM II operations.

The United States force introduced on December 9th was a model for deployment of a Joint Task Force (JTF). The command element had been designated by CENTCOM as I MEF and the commander was given units of I MEF, the United States Army's 10th Mountain Division, the 15th Marine Expeditionary Unit (MEU), carrier aviation from the USS Ranger Battle Group and intelligence and logistics assets from the Air Force and Army. These forces were consolidated under UNITAF after the attachment of participating United Nations forces. These forces included more than 17,000 troops from 20 countries, bringing the total force to approximately 28,000 troops.

UNITAF Planning

The UNITAF campaign planning began in earnest at Camp Pendleton on December 1st. The 10th Mountain Division began joint planning immediately, "we did launch three LNOs right away—as soon as we found out we were going and that I MEF at Camp Pendleton, California was going to be our higher headquarters."[26] The UNOSOM forces would be concentrated in Mogadishu and planning with them would wait until after D-Day. The intent was for a United States-led UNITAF, spearheaded by the 15th MEU on December 9th. The 15th MEU would begin the first phase and the remaining phases would be clarified once the Headquarters (HQ) element was in country.

---

[25] The United Nations, *The United Nations in Somalia 1992-1996* (New York: United Nations, 1996), 40-41.

[26] Major General Steven Lloyd Arnold, "Operation Restore Hope", interview by Major Robert W. Wright and Captain Drew R Meyerowich interview in *Oral History Interview RHIT JHT 048 US Army Center of Military History Washington D.C. and Joint History Team Somalia* (26 February 1993): 5.

The UNITAF commander, Lieutenant General R.B. Johnston, had the luxury of a clear mission and defined role. Johnston maintained a close relationship with Oakley. This allowed for UNITAF to use both military and political influence on Aideed and Ali Mahdi. "No formal guidelines were established for the Johnston-Oakley relationship[27]. Oakley's mission was to act as overseer and coordinator of all United States civilian activities in Somalia, to provide political advice to UNITAF, to act as liaison with United Nations special envoy Kittani and to work closely with the NGO community to get humanitarian operations moving."[28] On the other hand, Johnston was charged with the security of the operation. His objectives were to implement the four phases and turn the mission back over to the United Nations. The UNITAF forces were initially deployed to secure the airfield at Mogadishu and the port of Mogadishu. Once established at the airport, the forces would move to open lines of communication throughout the city.

The JTFs primary military force would be the 15th MEU. The MEU aviation combat element (ACE) was composed of a composite helicopter squadron, which included (12) CH-46E *Sea Knights*, (4) CH-53E *Super Stallions*, (4) AH-1W *Super Cobras* and (3) UH-1N *Iroquois*. This force would be augmented by the CVBG. The USS Ranger would be able to assume control of the airspace through the use of the E-2C *Hawkeye*. The Ranger would also have (3) F/A-18A/C *Hornet* and (2) F-14A *Tomcat* squadrons.[29] The Tomcats would prove useful to the JFC through the use of photoreconnaissance. The 10th Mountain Division would also arrive with significant

---

[27] Joint Warfighting Center, *Joint Task Force Commander's Handbook for Peace Operations* (Ft. Monroe, VA: Joint Warfighting Center, 1995), 35-47.
[28] Hirsh and Oakley, 50.
[29] For a complete description of a CVBG see *Jane's Fighting Ships* and *Jane's Aircraft of the World*

attack assets, primarily (24) AH-1F *Cobras* and (12) OH-58C/D *Kiowa Warriors*. The final attack assets would arrive from Camp Pendleton as part of the follow on force, which included (8)AH-1Ws and (6) UH-1Ns from Marine Aircraft Group-39 (MAG-39).

The role of the Joint Force Air Component Commander (JFACC) would be significant. The JFACC would be Colonel Michael Delong, USMC. Delong was serving as the G-3 3rd Marine Aircraft Wing (MAW) prior to being assigned as the JFACC. Delong was designated as the JFACC by Johnston. As stated earlier, the role of the JFACC during UNITAF would prove to be one of the most significant events of the operation. The lessons learned by the JFACC and the formation of the JFACC planning cell would be invaluable to the UNITAF commander.

UNITAF Initial Phase of Operations Ashore

On the 9th of December 1992, the 15th MEU conducted an unopposed landing on the beaches of Mogadishu. After the December 9th landing, the UNITAF mission spread out of Mogadishu and into the outlying areas. The 10th Mountain Division and units of the Canadian Army landed on the 13th of December at the former Soviet airfield of Baledogle situated 160km northwest of Mogadishu. A Joint Marine/Army force secured Baidoa on the 17th, located approximately 300 kilometers from Mogadishu. "Once Mogadishu and Baledogle were secured, United States Air Force and charter flights operated night and day to bring United States Marines and Army contingents as well as foreign units to Somalia."[30] The operation would break the country into 8 zones of operation. Within each of these zones, nations were assigned areas of responsibility (see enclosure 2), with each zone having a commander whom reported directly to Johnston in Mogadishu.

UNITAF Forces and Equipment

These United States troops were well prepared for the deployment to the Somali desert. The majority of the Marines from I MEF had either served in the Persian Gulf War or had conducted extensive desert training in the Mojave Desert. The United States Army's 10th Mountain Division, led by Major General Thomas M. Arnold, was a light infantry division with organic helicopter support. Arnold would serve as both Commander, U.S. Forces Somalia (USFORSOM), and as deputy to the United Nation Force Commander in Somalia after the UNTIAF mission became UNOSOM II.

The 10th Mountain Division, according to MG Arnold was well prepared for the rigors of Somalia. In an interview conducted at the Army HQ in Mogadishu in February of 1993 he concluded that, " the United States Army has a really great training program, it's multi-echeloned...the unit has completed two training deployment to the National Training Center (NTC)[31], three recent deployments to the Joint Readiness Training Center (JRTC)[32] and we continue to train, that is the way to sustain the training program".[33] MG Arnold would serve as the Commanding General Army Forces Somalia (AFOR) and Commanding General of the 10th Mountain Division.

The key element to the success of the 10th was their tactical mobility and airborne firepower. An attack helicopter battalion supported the 10th. This battalion was equipped with AH-1F Cobras and OH-58C/D scout helicopters. The AH-1Fs were equipped with forward-looking infrared sensors (FLIR) and laser targeted (AIM-1 IR laser) 20mm cannon. This gave the AH-1F a distinct advantage during night operations.

---

[30] Hirsh and Oakley, 63.
[31] The U.S. Army's National Training Center (NTC) is primarily used to train armor heavy forces.
[32] The U.S. Army's Joint Readiness Training Center (JRTC) is primarily used to train light forces.
[33] Arnold interview, 8.

The use of the FLIR and 20mm cannon allowed for engagements at ranges beyond small arms. It also allowed the AH-1Fs the ability to limit collateral damage when firing into urban areas. The OH-58 scout aircraft gave the commander both observation and light firepower. The OH-58, with its FLIR and laser designation capability can locate and laser designate targets for other platforms delivering laser-guided munitions. This was an important planning factor for the JTF. The need to reduce or limit the amount of collateral damage was a necessity. The 10th would not have their forces into theater until the 13th of December.

The United States Naval Task Force was comprised of the Amphibious Ready Group (ARG) and the Carrier Battle Group (CVBG). Colonel Gregory Newbold led the Marines of the 15th MEU and along with Navy SEALs was the primary landing force on the night of December 9th. Fighter and attack aircraft from the USS Ranger spearheaded the CVBG. The CVBG was diverted to the AOR prior to the 5th of December. The CVBG provided essential OAS for the landing and subsequent operations in Mogadishu. The CVBG provided F/A-18s and F-14s for both close air support (CAS) and armed reconnaissance. The F-14s also provided photoreconnaissance. The primary advantage of jet aircraft was their psychological effects on the Somalis. The JFACC would assume control of all air operations on the 10th of December at the airport in Mogadishu. The decentralized nature of air operations would become the strength and trademark of UNITAF.

The 15th MEU brought a very limited OAS capability. The MEUs 4 AH-1Ws and 3 UH-1Ns had weight and range limitations in the intense Somali desert. These OAS assets would be supported by the 15th of December by a light attack squadron (HMLA)

21

based at Camp Pendleton, California. The AH-1Ws would be limited by a lack of FLIR capability and the UH-1Ns were limited by ordnance payload capability. The OAS assets would be dedicated to MAGTF operations, and the JFACC would have little influence of rotary wing OAS operations. This again provided decentralized control of OAS.

Challenges to OAS in Urban Operations

The built up areas around Mogadishu would become a challenge for ordnance delivery if required. It was determined early in the planning that attack helicopters, as well as carrier based fixed wing attack aircraft would be required. The J5 of the JCS had considered the amount of collateral damage that traditional fire support causes. Though planning for the use of OAS was a consideration, it was not anticipated due to the nature of the mission. The temperature would increase the need for water and reduce the lift capacity of helicopters. Otherwise, the terrain outside of Mogadishu would support the direct and indirect fire weapons of UNITAF. The lines of communication were open due to the mobility of helicopters and the ability of vehicles to operate off of established roads. This gave UNITAF the ability to operate through the country primarily by using the airport at Mogadishu and relying on helicopters to provide interior supplies.

The most challenging and dangerous portion of the operation came once inside the city of Mogadishu and Kismayo. The urban environment causes a myriad of targeting and communications problems. Existing structures and the ROE often limit the use of indirect fire. The ability to communicate is often limited by the need for line of sight. The lack of reliable maps and non-standard traffic patterns within the city made it difficult for armored convoys to maneuver. The preferred method of patrol was the deployment of squad sized foot patrols. Planning by I MEF had considered the availability of and use of attack helicopters during ground operations. The UNITAF commander, with close coordination with Oakley, was concerned with the overuse of attack assets and the impact that it would have on the NGOs ability to accomplish their mission. Regardless of the humanitarian mission, the danger to ground patrols would be immense. The patrols were carrying only organic weapons and exposure to heavy weapons and sniper fire was a constant concern. Sniper threats were a concern for both UNITAF and UNOSOM II operations. The use of attack helicopters to counter snipers would have caused excessive collateral damage.

Enemy Threat to Airborne Operations

The Somali militias, primarily led by Aideed, were also easily able to blend in with the community. The militia members wore no military uniforms, but many did have formal military training under both Soviet and United States sponsorship. The Somalis had detailed knowledge of the urban environment, which gave them an inherent advantage. Conversely, the urban environment would provide the Somalis with significant tactical challenges. They had open access to the city but were limited in firepower and dependent upon neighborhood support. Local support would seem simple, but historical clan lines had made portions of the city off-limits to other clans. There were several firefights between the Marines and members of Aideed's militia within the first three days. The incidents proved to the Somalis that they should avoid firing at attack helicopters and Marines patrolling.

This program was repeated in the South as the 10th mountain Division sent units to secure Kismayo. The operation in the South faced similar challenges as those experienced in Mogadishu. The Somali militia was armed with an assortment of imported weapons. Somalia had no indigenous weapons or ammunition production capability. The majority of the weapons were imported illegally through Kenya into Kismayo and subsequently shipped to Mogadishu. This is another reason why it was important for Aideed to form and nurture relationships with allies in Kismayo. The 'technicals'[34] that patrolled Mogadishu were small truck or all terrain vehicles with mounted direct and indirect fire weapons. The majority of 'technicals' were mounted with Soviet supplied 12.7mm and 14.5mm machineguns and United States supplied 106mm recoilless rifles. These weapons were the primary heavy threat posed by the militias. The individual Somali fighter could be using anything from a newly imported Russian AK-47 to a United States supplied M-16. The strategic mission of the SNA and Aideed was to gain United Nations backing and regain power. This would require Aideed to negotiate with and accept aid from the United Nations. Aideed preferred that the United Nations give him the power to save Somalia. He was anticipating the departure of the United Nations, and portrayed himself as the savior of Somalia. This would not be the case. The SNA and Aideed would become increasingly focused on overpowering the UNOSOM forces to regain control of Mogadishu. Ali Mahdi was also contending for Mogadishu, but taking a less active role against UNOSOM. It can be said that Aideed was similar to Napoleon in that he would conduct operations though the entire spectrum of war. His operational plans would be characterized by the maturation of Somali public opinion. As UNITAF and the diplomatic mission led by Oakley forced Aideed to capitulate, he became more determined to undermine the UNITAF mission.

---

[34] A 'Technical' as defined as any vehicle capable of firing heavy machine guns, recoilless rockets or mortars. Somalis would typically use trucks with mounted machineguns welded into the bed as fighting vehicles. These vehicles were the first targets engaged by United States Marine and Army attack helicopters in December 1992 and January 1993.

The Somalis lacked formal lines of communication. Their principal method of communication was through runners. The Somalis lacked tactical mobility and communications along with a limited resupply capability. The SNA and Aideeds most significant communication device was the national radio station in Mogadishu. The militias also lacked significant resupply and had very little ability to maintain heavy equipment. Mogadishu had several weapons storage sights, which housed Soviet T-34 tanks and United States delivered M-48 tanks. These tanks were rendered combat ineffective due to years of neglect and were stripped of anything that could be reused or sold. The Somalis also had no airpower. This would only be significant if any of the abandoned aircraft at airfields at Kismayo, Mogadishu or Bardera were operational.

Logistics

One of the key strengths of UNITAF was their logistical support. The UNITAF immediately set up a combined logistics base. The United States had the ability to provide sealift, airlift and use preposition ships for support. The support was available inland through the use of Navy Seabees and the Army Corps of Engineers. "UNITAF units of the Army engineers and Seabees built or repaired 2,500 kilometers of roads, nine airfields able to handle C-130s, eighty-five helicopter pads, and more."[35] The operational mobility of airlift allowed for land based OAS assets to be continuously resupplied with parts, fuel and ammunition. Naval aviation was only limited by the number of parts and ammunition on board ship. The need for logistics support throughout UNITAFs operating bases required ground convoys to be escorted by attack helicopters.

UNITAF JFACC Execution

---

[35] Hirsh and Oakley, 67.

The UNITAF mission would be conducted according to the four-phase plan, which included: securing of the airport and port of Mogadishu, securing of areas inland, securing Kismayo and finally, transitioning the mission back to UNOSOM. Oakley had brought the Somalis to the negotiation table. Oakley and Johnston had also been very successful in creating effective working relationships with the NGOs through the formation of the civilian-military operations center (CMOC). The first phase had been successful, the airport and seaport of Mogadishu had been secured. This initial phase, carried out by Marines and SEALs of the 15th MEU, was completed by the 13th of December. The second phase, which included the securing of Baledogle and Baidoa with Marine, Army and United Nations forces, had been completed by the 13th of December. These initial phases had been conducted with notable speed and efficiency along with limited confrontation with Somali militias.

The UNITAF forces had completely overwhelmed the Somalis. The incorporation of the carrier battle group, along with Marine and Army aviation had been a significant psychological weapon. "The major impact of attack helicopters in the Somalia AOR was their psychological effect."[36] The size of the UNITAF force combined with armor and offensive air support was a significant deterrent to the Somalis. Somalis active in opposition to the UNITAF were, by December, generally cut into the two factions led by Aideed and Ali Mahdi. They had received ample warning and continuous briefings from the United Nations special envoy, Kittani and the United States special envoy Oakley. This proactive political stance would serve both UNITAF and the

---

[36] Commanding General 10th Mountain Division, subject: "US Army Forces, Somalia After Action Report Summary." (3 June 1993), 62.

Somalis. The envoys had articulated to Aideed and Ali Mahdi that the UNITAF forces would be given liberal ROE on their December 11th meeting.

The JFACC staff was prepared for operations by the 11th of December. The existing United Nations staff augmented the staff. The UNOSOM staff would have little impact in the planning of air operations. The importance of the UNSOM staff was in planning operations and processing requests for support. The largest challenge for the JFACC was the lack of airspace control and the lack of aviation support at the airfield in Mogadishu.[37] Approximately 6 hours after the BLT of the 15th MEU had gone ashore, the JFACC and the staff were ashore and coordinating OAS missions throughout the city.

The ability of the JFACC to execute shaping operations was key to UNITAF success. Shaping was conducted in a non-traditional sense by the continuous presence of OAS aircraft. These aircraft allowed the JTF commander the flexibility and mobility he needed to conduct the humanitarian mission on the ground. The U.S Army operates attack helicopter battalions as their primary OAS asset. The United States Army's independent operations would allow them to shape their battle space, in a similar non-traditional manner, as they saw appropriate. The JFACC would exercise little control United States Army helicopter operations. Shaping was critical to all of the area commanders. The southern region of Kismayo would benefit from the use of the attack battalions reach.

UNITAFs ability to shape their priority areas of operation through the use of OAS was demonstrated by naval aviation's use of F-14A from the CVBG conducting photoreconnaissance missions into central Somalia. This allowed them to identify supply movements and also map LOCs. The rotary wing aircraft from the MEU/ARG and MAG-16 (-) would secure airfields in Biadoa and Baledogle. These early shaping missions would establish a UNITAF presence to the local population and provide the commander a significant force multiplier.

The shaping mission and missions in direct support of ground operations were focused to support UNITAFs humanitarian mission. The JFACC focused the OAS support to contribute to the primary mission of humanitarian relief. The humanitarian mission was essential to the coalition. The member states were primarily concerned with the political ramifications of reducing the existing death rate verses having sufficient OAS assets to execute Chapter VII operations. The JFACC was manned entirely by United States personnel. The United Nations were offered positions on the staff, but since they had limited numbers of participating aircraft, they declined. The United Nations was offered missions available on the ATO. The JFACCs primary mission remained supporting the JTF commander. The JFACC began using 'push' tactics to support United Nations ground operations.

Ground operations of the United Nations were initially based around protection of humanitarian relief convoys. The JFACC, after the 12th of December, began assigning USMC AH-1Ws to conduct escort operations. The French, German and Italian forces had been experiencing theft of supplies and fuel.[38] Along with the theft of fuel bladders, several humanitarian relief convoys had been highjacked enroute from Mogadishu into

---

[37] Michael P. Delong, Lieutenant General, United States Marine Corps, Deputy Commander-in-Chief, United States Central Command, interview by author, 21 December 2000. Delong served as the JFACC for UNITAF.
[38] Delong interview.

south central Somalia. The JFACC was faced with a series of early challenges that limited their ability to correctly apply OAS assets.

JFACC limitations

The lack of navigational aids and tactical direction finding equipment for OAS assets cause the JFACC to depend on the sea based radars. The CVBG would have requests sent to them through the JFACC and the air tasking order (ATO). The aircraft would launch from either the CV or LPH and use the ship's radar until passed off to the Marine air support team located at the airfield in Mogadishu. All other flights attempting to get into Mogadishu would contact the Aegis cruiser and be passed off to the CV radar teams and finally to the air support detachment at Mogadishu. The JFACC also established SOPs for all participating aircraft entering and existing Mogadishu. These procedures included airspace restrictions issued through international notices to airman. These would be crucial in ensuring safe and efficient control of all aviation assets. These control procedures would be most crucial for requesting and receiving OAS assets.

The JFACC for UNITAF was operational 24 hours. In the initial phases of UNITAF operations, the ATO was responsible for processing 2500 sorties per day.[39] The use of the Marine Air Command and Control Squadron (MACCS) and the Marine Air Support Squadron (MASS) were essential to the effective use of OAS. The ability of the JFACC to establish and maintain a direct air support center (DASC) was essential for ground operations. The DASC was responsible for processing all immediate air requests. This gave the JFACC the ability to put sea borne and land based OAS and search and rescue (SAR) assets on strip alert status. The strip alert status allows for aircraft to be economized and optimized for combat operations. The lack of a JFACC and the command and control it brought to UNITAF will be highlighted in the UNOSOM II mission.

Except for several small engagements in Mogadishu, there was little armed opposition to the UNITAF forces that required OAS. What was significant and cannot be quantified was the impact of the presence mission of OAS assets. Aideed was content with moving his heavy weapons into the United Nations authorized cantonment areas or out of the city. Ali Mahdi also wanted to avoid direct conflict and moved his heavy weapons into cantonment areas or authorized weapons storage sites (AWSSs). Relative calm allowed time for observation by the Somalis of UNITAF military operations. Aideed and Ali Mahdi both continued to secretly import weapons through Kenya into caches located west and south of Mogadishu. It gave them time to observe and pattern UNITAF procedures and techniques.

Mini-Case Study: United States Army Attack Helicopter Operations in Kismayo

The most critical test of UNITAF presence came in the southern port city of Kismayo. The United States Army had been assigned to several of the eight zones, one of them Kismayo. Two factions controlled the city. General Morgan, the son-in-law of deposed Said Barre, led one faction and the other, Colonel Omar Jess, was an ally of Aideed. Morgan had nearly 1,000 men from the former Somali Army and Jess had only a militia formed from various clans. The United States Army had established the 10th Mountain Divisions Deputy, Brigadier General Magruder, as commander Task Force Kismayo and the UNITAF forces.

On January 24, 1993, Morgan's forces attacked SPM (Jess) units at Bir Hane, only thirty-five kilometers outside of Kismayo, where Jess's men had been quietly

---

[39] Delong interview.

guarding their heavy weapons in a UNITAF designated compound. Citing the Aideed

cease-fire agreement, signed but violated by Morgan's Somali National Front (SNF),

United States helicopter gunships and Belgian armor counterattacked the next day,

destroying a number of technicals and artillery pieces and forcing the SNF to withdraw

further into the bush.[40] The following day, Morgan's Somali National Front (SNF) had

units attacked by United States Army AH-1Fs with 20mm, 2.75" rockets and TOW

missiles[41]. A Belgian armored convoy operating out of the Port of Kismayo supported

the attack. The attack destroyed several 'technical' vehicles and artillery pieces. The

attacks were authorized by the JTF, which cited violations of the Addis Abba ceasefire

agreement.[42] These two days of OAS operations would be the last OAS mission

conducted by either UNITAF or UNOSOM II in Kismayo. The qualitative impact of

OAS in support of UNITAF can only be measured against UNOSOM II performance.

Transition from UNITAF to UNOSOM II

UNITAFs four phases operation was complete by mid-February 1993.

The JTF, Johnston, had articulated to both the United States and United Nations special

envoys that the transition to UNOSOM II or OPERATION CONTINUE HOPE was

ready to begin. The UNOSOM II forces would be consolidated under Lieutenant General

Bir from Turkey. The United Nations had planned to both reduce the force while

expanding the mission, to include disarmament of Somali clans. Both Oakley and

Johnston were adamant concerning the transition of power from the United States to the

United Nations. The longer the United States remained the lead, the longer assets would

---

[40] Hirsh and Oakley, 76-77.
[41] Commander 10th Mountain Division (Light Infantry), subject: "US Army Forces, Somalia After Action Report Summary," 02 June 1993, 61.

be drained in the operation. Once the United Nations took the lead they could begin 'nation building' steps that only the United Nations had the moral authority and international support to begin. The United States had agreed to leave behind a 1300 man quick reaction force with its associated OAS and assault support assets. Admiral Bowman of the JCS also explained to the United Nations Secretariat that the MEU would be available if needed.

This left the UNOSOM II forces significantly short of OAS assets. UNITAFs departure completely stripped away all fixed wing assets and left the limited United States Army and MEU aircraft. Equally important was the departure of UNITAFs JFACC and the mechanisms that could plan and execute ground operations with the necessary OAS. This limitation would be highlighted in the 5 June ambush of a Pakistani ground convoy. Another change that occurred with the transition from UNITAF to UNSOM II was the replacement of Oakley. Retired Admiral Jonathan Howe would replace Oakley. Howe worked as the Deputy National Security Advisor to President Bush and had been monitoring the changes during OPERATION RESTORE HOPE.

The transition from UNITAF to UNOSOM II would symbolize several key changes in the Somalia mission. The United States demanded that the United Nations assume the long-term leadership role. This was a role that the United Nations clearly was not ready to accept.[43] Oakley also articulated that the United Nations was responsible for the humanitarian mission and the United Nations must replace the United States on the military as well as the civilian side. These changes would change the nature of all military operations. Specifically, OAS operations would now be reactive in nature with

---

[42] For more on the Addis Abba Agreement see United Nations Operation in Somali from 1992-96, produced by the United Nations.

limited command and control of assets. Moreover, the Somalis would soon realize that without OAS, ground operations would be more vulnerable to interdiction and harassment. These changes, combined with the expanded mandate of the United Nations, would elongate the United Nations timeline.

The expanded role of UNOSOM II was mandated with United Nations Security Council Resolution 814 on March 26.[44] The replacement of the UNITAF forces with United Nations forces was a historical-setting event. This would be the first time in history that forces would be operating under Chapter VII of the United Nations charter. Two main objectives were assigned to UNOSOM II: Consolidation, expansion and maintenance of a secure environment throughout Somalia and rehabilitation of the political institutions and economy of Somalia. Howe would work hard to keep UNITAF in place until June, but both Johnston and Hoar articulated to the JCS that they had accomplished their assigned mission.

The new United Nations Commander, Lieutenant General Bir, had voiced concerns over the lack of air power. Without the direct leadership of the United States or a strong contingent of troops Bir would lack the necessary legitimacy and leverage to accomplish his mission.

UNOSOM II Operations

The transition from UNITAF to UNOSOM II would face a series of early challenges. However, most of the challenges would go unresolved. UNOSOM II lost its ability to command and control air sets once the JFACC departed. They also lost the majority of their fixed and rotary wing OAS assets. The CVBG had departed by March

---

[43] For more on the transition from UNITAF to UNOSOM II see Hirsh and Oakley or *The Blue Helmets*.
[44] United Nations, 301.

and May only a United States Army attack battalion (-) was remaining. UNOSOM II also lost all of its assault support helicopters and was forced to seek civilian contracts.

The final phase of UNITAF was the transfer to UNOSOM II. UNSOM II began to implement their 4-phased plan: transition to UNOSOM II, consolidation and expansion (disarmament), transfer to civilian authority and redeployment.[45] The passing of United Nations Security Council resolution 837 called for the more active role in disarmament by UNOSOM II forces. The marked reduction of United States forces, combined with the reduction of UNOSOM II ground patrols, led to increase clan operations. Both Ali Mahdi and Aideed would maintain low profiles during the transition period. This allowed them both opportunities to increase their local support base and continue to import weapons from Kenya.

A critical link for them was their ties to the South. Though the southern clans had avoided confrontation with UNITAF forces after the gunship attacks, they continued to provide support. To counter this, in mid-February, the special envoys and Johnston would order Jess and Morgan out of Kismayo. Morgan was sent to the Kenyan border village of Doubly.

United States transition to UNOSOM II

This was a period of considerable intelligence gathering by the Somalis. The UNITAF forces were departing throughout February and by March only portions of the United States Army's 10th Mountain, I MEF HQ, portions of MAG-16 (-) and the 24th MEU were available. The distant lack of OAS assets was a concern for both Johnston

---

[45] "UNOSOM II OPERATION CONTINUE HOPE Peacemaking" informational brief, n.p., n.d., provided on 20 December 2000 by Brigadier General R.F. Natonski, 4-11. Natonski received this as part of his transition brief while serving as the BLT ½ commander with the 24th MEU during transition from UNITAF to UNOSOM II.

and Bir. Both were aware of the limitations of the UNOSOM II forces. Yet, neither would be able to predict the deadly consequences, which would follow once credible OAS assets departed.

"The Marines of the 24th MEU, under the command of Colonel Matthew Broderick, would arrive in late February and ensure the removal of Morgan's forces."[46] The southern AOR was turned over to the 24th MEU, along with the Belgian forces already in place.[47] The success in the South would lead, by mid-February 1993, the UNITAF leadership to begin the final transition phase of OPERATION RESTORE HOPE. The successful integration and decentralized use of OAS, primarily rotary wing, had given the JTF commander control of not only the cities but also the outlying areas. These outlying areas had been responsible for harboring weapons storage sites and militia leaders. The success of the operation to date was based on a series of planning successes. The ability of the United States project forces on both the ground and in the air was instrumental in bringing the Somalis to the bargaining table. The ability of UNITAF to form a cohesive military unit under a single commander made operations synchronized at the operational level. UNITAF clearly had better trained, educated and equipped military forces. These forces would also distinguish themselves through the restraint of force[48].

The rules of engagement (ROE) that had been formulated by the JTF commander had provided the needed flexibility and favored UNITAF forces. Throughout UNITAF there are countless examples where tactical restraint proved to ease tensions between

---

[46] David Bowne Wood, *A Sense of Values: American Marines in an Uncertain World* (Kansas City: Andrews and McMeel, 1994), 39-40.
[47] Richard F. Natonski, Brigadier General, United States Marine Corps, interviews by author, 18 and 20 December 2000. Natonski served as the BLT ½ commander with the 24th MEU during OPERATION RESTORE AND CONTINUE HOPE (UNITAF/UNOSOM II).
[48] Canadian Army forces were involved a ROE incident in Baidoa, see Canadian Army After Action.

Somali non-combatants and UNITAF forces. These factors combined with the ability of the United Nations and United States special envoy to establish a close relationship with the NGOs and the belligerent allowed the military arm to conduct an operational campaign unfettered by bureaucratic constraints and restraints.

UNSOM II OAS Limitations

The UNOSOM II OAS assets through June of 1992 were primarily the AH-1s from the 10th Mountain and the AV-8B *Harriers* and AH-1Ws from the 24th MEU. There was no command and control at the UNOSOM II level. Bir's staff had no standing JFACC and had no established procedures to effectively coordinate requests. The airport was still under the control of United Nation and United States controllers, but the infrastructure to process and coordinate any type of OAS was lost.

The 10th Mountain had used their OAS assets as an independent maneuver element and had not been heavily tasked by the JFACC during UNITAF. The JFACC had primarily concerned itself with naval OAS assets. The Marines had coordinated the use of attack helicopters as part of the JFACCs air tasking order (ATO). UNOSOM II would only indirectly have the 24th MEUs AV-8Bs as fixed wing assets[49]. The MEU was not a participating UNOSOM II force member; they were attached to the QRF[50]. The AV-8Bs did have the ability to conduct long-range visual reconnaissance through the use

---

[49] The United States would also provide AC-130U *Specter* gunships. These aircraft were based in Mombassa, Kenya and under the direct control of the QRF and later Task Force Ranger commander. The after action reports of the AC-130s are classified and do not provide significant lessons learned to this study.

[50] The United States role was conceived in terms of logistical support and along with the QRF would operate under the tactical control of the Commander, U.S. Forces Somalia, Major General Thomas Montgomery. The mission was as follows: When directed, UNOSOM II forces Command conducts military operations to consolidate, expand, and maintain a secure environment for the advancement of humanitarian aid, economic assistance and political reconciliation in Somalia.

of their heads-up-display cameras. This information provided the MEU commander and the QRF commander raw data on large convoy movements coming from Kenya.

The lack of an integrated air picture was a major limitation to the UNOSOM II staff. The lack of OAS assets combined with the expanded mandate would frustrate UNSOM II. The United States Army would begin to remove all of their assets from outside Mogadishu by May of 1993. They would consolidate and support UNOSOM II from the airport. The 24th MEU would depart in July of 1993, a departure highlighted by an attempt to capture Aideed. Aideed was considered the catalyst of the 5 June attack of a Pakistani ground patrol that left more than 25 KIA.

The United States Army and the USAF would be the primary providers of OAS after July of 1993. The expanded mission of UNOSOM II would lead the United States to begin a campaign of retribution against Aideed. This campaign included extensive use of OAS assets in the search of and attempts to capture Aideed and his closest lieutenants. That campaign goes well beyond the scope of this study[51]. Once the 5 October mission had been completed, additional MEUs flowed into Somalia (13th and 22nd). The 13th MEU, under the command of Colonel Lawrence Outlaw arrived in late October.

Once again the aviation picture was difficult to discern due to the lack of a JFACC or any type of OAS planning by the UNOSOM II staff. There were no formal command and control procedures for land and naval-based OAS assets. The 13th MEU ACE commander, Lieutenant Colonel Leif Hendrickson, coordinated with the United States Army attack battalion commander Lieutenant Colonel Lee Gore for deconfliction. The United Nations officers were indifferent to aviation operations and did little to

---

[51] To learn more about the 5 October 1993 mission of Task Force Ranger and the 160th Special Operations Aviation Regiment, see *BlackHawk Down* by Mark Bowen.

coordinate. The United States assets were assigned the 'eyes over Mogadishu' mission, which was a 24-hour visual reconnaissance mission[52]. United States Forces Somalia (USFORSOM) assigned this mission.

Mini-Case Study: 5 June 1993

UNOSOM IIs expanded mandate met with immediate and deadly results. UNOSOM II faced serious command and control issues. These issues went well beyond coordinating a comprehensive air campaign to support their expanded mission. The expanded mission was not completely embraced by the member nations and many members refused UNOSOM missions. This lack of control was exacerbated by the permanent assignment of sectors. Each nation was given a geographic region within Mogadishu. This led to local brokering between clans and nations. This also accelerated the credibility gap between UNOSOM II and Ali Mahdi and Aideed.

The Pakistani government had provided the initial land force for UNOSOM in the fall of 1992. They had maintained an active patrolling regiment through the city. On 5 June, during a routine patrolling operation a Pakistani patrol came under small arms fire. Following UNOSOM II ROE they pursuer the attackers into a pre-planned Somali prepared ambush site. The Pakistanis were engaged with heavy weapons and RPG-7s. Several of their APCs were destroyed. The Pakistanis soon ran low of small arms ammunition[53]. Several were captured and executed, while others managed to escape and return to the airport.

---

[52] Leif H. Hendrickson, Brigadier General, United States Marine Corps, President of Marine Corps University, interview by author, 20 December 2000. Hendrickson served as the Commanding Officer of Marine Medium Helicopter Squadron (Reinforced)-268 attached to the 15th MEU in October of 1993.
[53] Sinai, 287-92.

This incident was not without prior warnings. UNOSOM II had been pressuring Aideed and his supporters to cease radio broadcast and prevent them from removing weapons from their AWSS (authorized weapons storage sites). UNOSOM II had not coordinated the patrol, nor had they any means to provide OAS assets. UNSOM II had not initiated any plans to integrate U.S Army AH-1s in ground operations, not had they conducted any Combined training. The Pakistanis did not have not forward air controllers who could speak English nor did the United States Army have foreign speaking pilots. This incident could have been repeated throughout the city. It led to the beginning of USFORSOMs campaign to capture Aideed.

Comparative Aviation Lessons learned

Throughout the operations in Somalia, commanders were forced to make decision that would ultimately lead to escalation. The use of OAS assets needs to be understood and weighed, as does any military option. The use of OAS assets matured from a traditional role to a non-traditional role of presence within UNITAF. UNOSOM II desired to use OAS in the traditional role while lacking the understanding of air-ground operations. The expanded mandate of UNSOM II and the more liberal ROE required OAS to be used in both the traditional non-traditional roles, but they were unable to accomplish either.

The nature of the conflict in Somalia dictated the decentralized use of OAS. Both the MAGTF of I MEF and the 10th Mountain Division were best served with command of their own assets. It became apparent of the importance of aviation after the UNITAF mission became that of UNOSOM II.

The planning conducted by the JFACC in UNITAF and the close coordination and support that OAS platforms require could not be duplicated by UNOSOM II. The use of OAS assets for UNITAF was designed to be adequate in accordance with the ROE and the aircrew was given specific training.[54] Though OAS assets exceedingly played a role of presence for UNITAF the planning and execution of missions followed the doctrinal lines formed through the use of the JFACC.

UNITAF was able to coordinate their requirement for OAS through the JFACC or though the direct tasking of subordinate units, if available. The JFACC went through significant maturing as the operation grew in size and complexity. The ATO would be coordinated by the Airspace Control Agency (ACA), as a special staff function, acting as a clearing house for publishing the flight schedule of fixed wing aircraft and establishing procedures for airspace control and deconfliction.[55] The Marines that would initially establish the ACA at Mogadishu would be replaced by the J-3 Air staff. The USAF would have both the tools and the personnel to best operate.[56]. This support network would continue to erode during UNOSOM II.

UNOSOM II had very little ability to control airspace and relied almost entirely on the United States to provide support. Also, UNOSOM II would require very centralized planning for OAS missions. These OAS missions consisted exclusively of US Army AH-1 and USAF AC-130Hs. The UNOSOM II OAS missions were coordinated through the J-3 staff and also went through the entire UNOSOM II staff and ultimately to the quick reaction force (QRF) commander Major General Montgomery,

---

[54] *Operation Restore Hope Lessons Learned Report*, Center for Army Lessons Learned, Fort Leavenworth, Kansas, Noveber, XIV 11-XIV 16.

[55] Katherine A. W. McGrady, The Joint Task Force in Operation Restore Hope, CRM 93-114 (Alexandria VA: Center for Naval Analysis, March 1994), 58.

USA or to the Joint Special Operations Task Force (JSOTF) located in Mombassa, Kenya.[57]

The use of OAS assets in the urban environment is challenging, but invaluable to the commander. The UNITAF mission was a success due to the pre-mission planning and a known end-state. Combined with the UNITAF ground scheme of maneuver for relief convoys, the use of the JFACC and OAS assets as a presence was crucial in the establishment of secure routes. OAS assets were also instrumental in keeping the warring clans factions restrained. Additionally, the use of OAS as a presence was done with the political savvy of Oakley. The UNITAF mission had both the political legitimacy and military might to influence Somali leaders.

In Hindsight, UNOSOM II began operations with an unattainable goal. The mission creep that plagued UNOSOM II led them to design OAS missions, which attempted to force Somali leadership, primarily Aideed, to capitulate. Both the nature of the conflict and political factors limited effectiveness. The UNOSOM II leadership and their respective national leadership did not have the resolve to pursue a cohesive strategy for Somalia. The seeming insensitivity of UNOSOM II to cause excessive collateral damage with OAS and ground assets would cause a major down swing in public opinion. The inability of UNOSOM II to understand the limitations of OAS was critical. The use of such excessive power at the lower ends of the conflict spectrum led to the Somali backlash.

---

[56] Joint Universal Lessons Learned Systems Reports 61051-22697 and 33407, 3rd MAW, June 1993.
[57] For more information on the use of the AC-130H or the 16th Special Operation Squadron (SOS) see their web site, www.af.mil and search under units. This site provides weapons and a limited historical description of missions flown in Somalia.

UNITAF and UNOSOM II Significance

The UNITAF campaign can be viewed as a model for successful United Nations intervention under Chapter VII. The campaign was successful at stopping the violence in Mogadishu and most of southern Somali Somalia. The United Nations was able to provide aid that saved an estimated 3 million lives. UNITAFs successful operational campaign would place a large burden on UNOSOM II. UNITAF took a large step in the direction of rebuilding Somalia.

The rebuilding of Somalia would be left up to UNOSOM II. Unfortunately, UNOSOM II would not benefit from the leadership or resources enjoyed by UNITAF. The Somalis would learn quickly that the UNOSOM II forces were unable to either contain or restrain militia forces. The United States military mission under UNITAF was designed to stop the violence, under Chapter VII, while allowing for humanitarian operations to continue. UNOSOM II would attempt to build on the success of UNITAF and expand their role into disarming the militias and undertake nation building.

Future Implications

The significant lessons learned from UNITAF begin with an examination of the current foreign policy under former President Bush. The Powell Doctrine had demanded that United States forces not be committed without a clear entry and exit strategy along with deploying the proper force structure. UNITAF was successful on both counts; the deployment of United States forces in support of Operation Restore Hope passed the Powell Doctrine and answered the call of American idealists and realists, Republicans and Democrats and the international community. The use of a CMOC to integrate the NGO, military, United Nation and Somali leadership was effective. Strong leadership

42

and flexibility was evident through the Johnston and Ambassador Oakley relationship. This relationship may be seen as a limitation due to Oakley and Johnston's perceived power by the Somalis; it may have worked to undermine the United Nations.

The Somalis were able to observe the operations of the United Nations and the United States military throughout the six months of UNITAF operation. The Somalis would soon take advantage of their lessons learned after the UNITAF handoff to UNOSOM II. The Somalis would also take advantage of the perceived weakness of non-United States forces. This was witnessed in the June 5th 1993 ambush and subsequent killing of 25 Pakistani peacekeepers.

The lessons learned by UNITAF were quickly forgotten by UNOSOM II. The force would consistently exceed its limitations. UNOSOM II failed to take advantage of the established CMOC. This would lead to mistrust between the Somalis and the United Nations. The political planning would break down and individual nations began ignoring the commands of the UNOSOM commander and relied on orders from home. The smaller UNOSOM II force would allow the Somalis to reclaim stored weapons, which led to attacks against rival clans and the United Nations. The limited use of air support would give the Somalis unobserved freedom of movement. UNOSOM II would also limit the number of ground patrols and virtually eliminate night patrols. UNOSOM II mistakenly would only leave their compounds in force to engage militia forces. This would continue to erode any confidence the Somali people had in the United Nations. UNITAFs legacy should be one of success, an operational campaign that saved a decaying United Nations mission from failure. Instead, it is generally viewed as part of the overall failure of the United Nations mission in Somalia.

Bibliography

Allard, Kenneth, *Somalia Operations: Lessons Learned*. Washington, D.C.: National Defense University Press, 1995.

"Appendix 6 to Annex C to UNOSOM II OPLAN 1, Rules of Engagement" informational brief, 0221200C May 1993, provided on 20 December 2000 by Brigadier General R.F. Natonski, C-6-1-3.

Arnold, Steven Llyod, Major General USA. *Operations Restore Hope: Interview RHIT JHT 048 by Major Robert W. Wright and Captain Drew R. Meyerowich*. Washington, D.C.: US Army Center of Military History, 1993.

Baker, Caleb. "Manhunt for Aideed: Why the Rangers Came Up Empty Handed," *Armed Forces Journal,* December 1993, 18.

Bowen, Mark. *BlackHawk Down*. Philadelphia: University of Pennsylvania Press, 1997.

Center for Army Lessons Learned. *Operation Restore Hope Lessons Learned Report*. Fort Leavenworth, Kansas: Center for Army Lessons Learned, 1994.

Commanding General 10th Mountain Division, *US Army Forces, Somalia: After Action Report Summary*. Fort Drum, NY: Department of the Army, 1993.

Delong, Michael P. Lieutenant General, United States Marine Corps, Deputy Commander-in-Chief, United States Central Command. Interview by author, 21 December 2000.

Fleck, Dieter. *The Handbook of Humanitarian Law in Armed Conflict*. New York: Oxford Press, 1995.

Hendrickson, Leif H. Brigadier General, United States Marine Corps, President of Marine Corps University. Interview by author, 20 December 2000.

Hirsh, John and Oakley, Robert. *Somalia and Operation Restore Hope*. Washington, D.C.: United States Institute for Peace, 1995.

Joint Publication 1-02, DOD Dictionary of Military and Associated Terms, 1998.

Joint Universal Lessons Learned Systems Reports 61051-22697 and 33407, 3rd MAW, June 1993.

Joint Warfighting Center. *Joint Task Force Commander's Handbook for Peace Operations*. Ft. Monroe, VA: Joint Warfighting Center, 1995.

Libutti, Frank. Lieutenant General, United States Marine Corps, Commanding General Marine Forces Pacific. Interview by author, 8 December 2000.

Makinda, Samuel M. *Seeking Peace from Chaos: Humanitarian Intervention in Somalia.* Boulder, CO: Lynee Rienner Publishers, 1993.

McGrady, Katherine A. W. *The Joint Task Force in Operation Restore Hope.* Alexandria VA: Center for Naval Analysis, March 1994.

MCRP 5-12C, Marine Corps Supplement to the DOD Dictionary of Military and Associated Terms, 1997.

MCRP 5-12D, Organization of Marine Corps Forces, 1998.

Natonski, Richard. Brigadier General, United States Marine Corps. Interview by author, 18 and 20 December 2000.

Simma, Bruno. *The Charter of the United Nations.* New York: Oxford Press, 1995.

Sinai, Joshua. *United Nations Peacekeeping: Lessons Learned.* Washington, D.C.: Library of Congress, 1994.

United Nations, *The United Nations in Somalia, 1992-1996.* NY: Department of Public Information, 1996.

United Nations. *The Blue Helmets 3rd Edition.* New York: United Nations, 1997.

"UNOSOM II OPERATION CONTINUE HOPE Peacemaking" informational brief, n.p., n.d., provided on 20 December 2000 by Brigadier General R.F. Natonski, 4-11.

Wood, David Bowne. *A Sense of Values: American Marines in an Uncertain World.* Kansas City: Andrews and McMeel, 1994.